THIS PRAYING THING

By the same author

AND THIS IS JOY

A SONG FOR ALL SEASONS

THIS PRAYING THING

by

JOY WEBB

with drawings by
Alf Ward

HODDER AND STOUGHTON

LONDON SYDNEY AUCKLAND
TORONTO

This Praying Thing

I suppose someone, somewhere has got it all wrapped up ...
This praying thing ...
But it's not me!
If I were called on to pray in public
I think I'd die ... honestly—
Or if I didn't die, I'd clam-up and stutter out
Some stupid things I'd heard other folk say
And it wouldn't really be me!

I've heard folk say that praying is just like having a
    conversation with You—
But I'm not much good at making conversation either—
Especially with people I don't know,
And I sometimes feel I don't know You very well,
Really!

There are lots of things I don't like about praying, actually!
For instance—
I don't like it when people sound as tho' they've got it all
    rehearsed and off pat!
You must have noticed, surely!
But then—
I don't much care for the over chatty types;
That doesn't seem very natural to me, either,
At least, not in public!
So You see the problem ...
It looks as tho' I've got to find my own way to You!

Do You know how I'd like to think of it?
I'd like to think of it as 'coming home'...
You know how it is?
If you want to talk—you do!
If you don't . . . you don't!
And everyone understands!

Could it be like that between me and You?
That wherever I am
Whenever my thoughts turn to You,
You would count that as prayer?
Because if it wasn't a difficult thing
I think it would happen more often!

Introduction

A FEW MONTHS AGO a young teenager came into my office obviously wanting to talk. Now this, of course, is not an unusual occurrence; in fact I sometimes think my office is mistaken for an Advice Bureau. However, that's another story. What did interest me were her next words. 'You see,' she said, 'it's not the Bible and all that, that worries me . . . it's this praying thing!'

'This . . . praying . . . thing!' No, I suppose it's not a terribly reverent way of describing the greatest privilege a human being can experience : personal communication with God. But I liked one thing about it. It sounded as though it belonged to today, and it obviously meant something for her.

So that is the spirit in which I offer this collection of prayers. They belong to today, and today's world and society; and I hope that they will have meaning for you — today's young Christian. You see, ever since the germ of the idea of a book of prayers took root in my mind, I have been consciously observing you.

I've watched you think, feel, and react, and the way you generally tackle life. I've seen you excited, amused, pleased with yourselves, and I've seen you disappointed, disillusioned, hurt, let-down and bewildered. I've tried to cope with your questionings, some of your shouts about life and the 'older generation'.

Two things have crystallized in my mind about you. One is that many of you are obviously searching for a real faith. You are not prepared to assume, without question, the faith of your parents. You need to fashion your own reasons for believing —and I like this.

The second thing is that I've watched so many of you, in great sincerity missing the mark! You see, it's a hard fact, but the real Christian life doesn't only consist of great moments when you feel very inspired and responsive to God and the best in yourself; it's also got to do with Monday morning feelings, out-of-sorts days, and other people whom you don't particularly 'click with'. It has—you know!

You can't pre-package the spiritual life and preserve it beautiful and intact for Sundays. It won't be contained like this. It insists on spilling over into the real life and experience that is common or garden—everyday. And that is just where some of you have got to come to terms with it. Your life with God has to invade your every conscious moment . . . and that's where this praying thing comes in.

After all, what's the use of feeling greatly helped by a sermon on thoughtfulness on Sunday, and getting on everybody's nerves on Monday morning? Or collecting passionately for political refugees or some other 'good cause' and letting your own money slip through your fingers like water? It doesn't really add up, does it?

Praying, if it is anything, is a non-stop God-consciousness. And that is the atmosphere I hope you will discover in this book. I've only tried to capture that atmosphere in words, because that is one of the ways human beings express themselves and, let's face it, that is the only way that I, personally, can reach you.

Do use the 'Shout Prayers' too. If you're like me, you'll have to! God wants to be involved with that too! I hope you'll find you can add to the 'Thank You Prayers' also. Well, do it! I know I haven't exhausted the possibilities there.

When I look at the manuscript, four personalities seem to emerge. The first pair are in their mid-teens, a boy and a girl; then there is an older couple, say in their early twenties. You'll discover them for yourselves and, who knows, perhaps you're there too! I wouldn't be surprised.

Contents

III ME – AND MY RELATIONSHIPS

VI   SHOUT PRAYERS

VII   THANK YOU PRAYERS

I

The Way Things Are

I think a lot about
The way things are . . .
About Life, and living !
I know I can't change them
But would You help me to understand,
And accept them, please !

I'd like to make the most of it all, too,
(If that's not too much
To ask of You !).

1. The Sunshine Day

Oh, it's a gorgeous day ! Just wonderful !
Clear, clear blue sky—brilliant sunshine,
And just that touch of a nip-in-the-air
That makes me want to be free to walk and walk
And walk.

If I were a poet I could write a thousand poems today—
Or take a brush and capture for ever the clear blue-gold
    that is now !

Actually, I'm singing—a little off-key perhaps,
But singing,
Because I want You to know that this kind of day
Makes me glad to be alive,
Living,
Breathing—full of awareness !
So, listen—please !

2. On A Funny Day

It's a funny day today!
A kind of 'neither-one-thing' and 'neither-the-other'
Sort of day.
I don't know what to do with myself;
If only something would happen—
Something interesting, stimulating, amusing . . .
But it's not a 'happening' day.

It occurs to me that I can cope with those kind of days;
What I can't do is cope with the ordinary, run of the mill,
Today, kind of day!

Help me with the ordinary things—please.
Don't let me grow into a person always looking for
Ways to be entertained into finding life interesting!
Because I know that's a pretty poor kind of person;
A person who is bored with life is pathetic.

Don't let it happen to me—please!
Help me to find the interesting
In the ordinary!

3. Winter

I don't like winter!
Getting up on a bitter cold morning
In the dark;
Coming home at night
In the dark;
It's not my idea of living.

The trees are bare—starkly bare!
Not the slightest suspicion of a leaf
To give the clue that life is there.
And yet it is there, sleeping perhaps?

I guess I look like a permanent winter to You
Sometimes.
Stark and colourless
With not the merest hint of budding leaves
To clothe the awkwardness that is me,
The real me!

I need the Springtime of Your love in my life.
Warm me!

4. *One of My Moments*

I had one of my moments today—
You know . . . one of those, clear, bright, 'stripped'
   moments !
Everything suddenly moved into focus
And I knew, without a shadow of a doubt,
That our world and our destinies,
Are in Your Hand.
That what we do, and think, and feel
Is important,
That what we are, and try to become
Has meaning—
Not only for ourselves, but for others—
And for You !

I should have liked to hold on to that moment,
But it passed—as I knew it would;
Somehow tho', I feel stronger for it.
After all, in that moment I knew, really knew—
Life took on wide, wide horizons;
And although I can't always see them
I remember that they are there !

Thank You for that moment !
When I'm confused
Help me to remember !

5. What's It All About?

This morning I suddenly dropped into a mood where
I really started to wonder about things!
You know how it is.
Something starts you off on a train of thought
And away you go ...
Well, with me, it was just the news!
I was in the bathroom, actually—
And the transistor was playing
(In the background)
Then suddenly 'News time'
And my attention was captured.

My mind floated off ...
Whatever kind of world is this—anyway?
Where on earth are we going?
How is it that all the worst things seem to gain the
    headlines?
Only occasionally can they raise three cheers for the
    goodies!
Has this always been so?
Or is it worse, now that we have communication systems
That mean we can know about these things
Instantly—or at least
Every day.
Instead of perhaps, once a week,
Or month ... or six months?

But then (my mind said to me)—
Would I really want to live in a kind of
Cushioned state?
Knowing all kinds of things were happening
All over the world
Without me knowing about them—at all?

So, I'm stuck with this constant intrusion
Of the news, aren't I?
And on Monday morning
At 7 o'clock.
In the bathroom—
Listening to the transistor—
It's hard to remember
That You are over all!

6. Simply Trusting

D'You know . . .
My Gran's just great!
Whenever we have a family crisis
And everyone is up to '99
(Which is quite often, as we're pretty hectic as families go!)
She just quietly moves amongst us,
In the middle of all the din, and talk, and argument—
And if you ask her how she feels about it
She invariably replies—
'Simply trusting'!

I must say, I think she's great!
I really envy her poise and calm.
Do You think it might turn out to be hereditary?
(You haven't seen the signs yet?
No, well I suppose not, but I'm doing my best!)

Seriously,
I would like You to help me to learn about it—
'Simply trusting' I mean!
It would help in any more 'aerated' moments,
Wouldn't it?

7. The Bonus of Beauty

There are times when
There just aren't any words ...
Nothing you could say
Would express what you feel!
Beauty—in any form, really—
Does that to me!

I saw the most perfect sunset tonight,
And I thought
What right have we to this bonus
You have given us?
What have I ever done, or been,
To make that sunset mine, by rights?
Nothing!

So, I just let it fill my life
And somehow refresh my spirit!

Was that right?

8. Acceptance

Marie was chosen Head Girl today.
It might have been me—
I know I was on the short list.

Do You know—
A year ago this would have shattered me
For ages !
That fact that I'd been considered, and not chosen—
It would have been . . . too much !
But now, well, I'm learning to accept things.
(My Gran used to say that 'acceptance'
Was one of the most important words in the English
    language.
I guess she had something there !)

All I know is
It makes life an awful lot smoother,
And me a nicer person.
I'm not for ever straining at something beyond me,
I'm learning to live with what's possible.

D'You know . . . I'm encouraged about all this !
(Yes, I thought You would be, too !)

9. Books

I was in the library today,
Sitting in that deathly hush
That I usually manage to shatter!
I sat still, taking in the atmosphere,
The slightly musty smell of the books.
(I was swotting some ancient stuff!)

Suddenly I found myself thinking ...
About all the men and women
Whose life-thoughts were probably
Captured inside the covers of those books!
Of all the effort they represented,
But not only that—
All the learning, the acquired knowledge,
And original thinking married together
To produce new ideas
And fresh interpretations of old ones!
What a very special thing this was!

Thank You for that moment!
Books are a tremendous privilege,
Aren't they?

10. Laughter

Thank You for laughter—
It changed my world, today!

I was harassed and all 'put-about';
My day had gone completely 'up the creek':
I seemed to be fighting time
Single handed.
Suddenly, floating up from the flat below
And in through my open window
Where I was sitting working at my thesis,
Came the sound of children
Laughing!
A clear, delightful sound.
I looked out
And there they were,
These little girls
Playing with a kitten.

It 'saved the day' for me.
Thank You ...
And the children!

11. Love

You know—
I've a feeling that this word 'love'
Is in mortal danger !
Don't You think so ?
It seems to me that we can make it mean
Anything we want it to mean.

Take any song in the current Top Ten;
I guarantee you won't find two
That take the same slant on 'true love'.
Oh, I know that love between a man and a woman
Is only one kind of loving—but even so
I would have thought there would be a basic norm
Even in this, wouldn't You?
But it doesn't seem so, does it?

Do You think we're cheapening it? Lessening its value?
Do You think we could get to the stage where
We've devalued it so much
That it doesn't mean anything, anymore?
It's a bit 'scarey', isn't it?

I hope You'll take a hand in it, somewhere.
But I guess You'll say I ought to do something about it—
Myself ! (Yes . . . I thought so !)

12. The 'In' World

What do You think about this 'in' world
That we young ones have created?
Is it a valid world?
Will it help us cope with the wide world of living
That is waiting for us in the future?

Dad says that we're all going to have to
Snap out of it, some day.
(The sooner the better, he usually adds.)
Get our hair cut (I ask You!)—
Put on sensible clothes
And get down to some hard work.
Poor old Dad!
He can't get it into his head
That you can be serious about life
In anything else but a pinstriped suit.

Now Mum, on the other hand, says
'Young folk have always been the same'
And reminds him of the drain-pipe trousers
He used to wear when they were courting!
(Good old Mum!)

On the other hand . . .
If I'm honest
There are moments when I'm just a bit worried!
We seem to have made our 'in' world so watertight!

People on the outside can't get in—that is—
Unless they wear the right clothes—use the right
   language—
Act like we do !
And I find myself wondering, sometimes, whether those
   of us 'inside'
Will always be able to get out, again !

Since I've been working I've begun to realize
That it's all a bit of a pretend really.
It's a great thing to have going :
Everybody wearing the same things, talking the same things,
Interested in the same things . . .
Well, frankly, life is not like that, is it ?
People are different.
They dress differently,
Think differently,
Use different language to express themselves !
Do You know . . .
I think . . .
I like it that way ! I'd like to join !
But I'm a bit afraid of it.
That's why I stay where I am
In our little 'in' world,
And lots of others with me.

13. *Your Beautiful World (1)*

Your world! So beautiful,
It hurts me!
I cannot absorb it all—
My mind stretches to its limit
Yet remains so far from understanding;
But I can sense it,
Feel it,
Enjoy it,
And form my word of thankfulness—
Or (if You like) . . .
Praise!

14. Your Beautiful World (2)

Your world is so beautiful . . .

An aged person smiled at me—
The parchment skin creased into
A thousand beautiful wrinkles—
And then . . .
The wide calm eyes of a child
Blue and pure (and asking too)
Were turned on me, in question!
Afterwards
I watched the blazing, red, courage
Of a young mother
Coping with a spastic child
With unconscious beauty!

15. *Your Beautiful World (3)*

Your world is so beautiful ...

A door—open;
On the floor, around the bench
The wood shavings had fallen
In glorious abandon—
Curled and crisp and clean;
A wholesome sight.
Or remember ...
The strange nostalgic feel
Of a hearth fire;
Bright flames dropping to a glow
As the night wears on,
And I sit and see
The pictures in the fire,
Dreaming.
Or feel ...
Snow on a winter morning
Bright, white, untrodden.
A clear, crisp world
Waiting for my footsteps
To be first!

16. Your Beautiful World (4)

Your world is so beautiful ...

I saw the stark, sharp patterns of a steel works
Thrusting upwards, angular,
A dark, dark shape, against the night
Lit by its satanic furnace glow,
A strange, macabre beauty !
And ...
I have watched the sea,
A ranging, restless creature !
Leaping at the shores—
Lashing the breakwaters—
Snarling around the tiny boats, anchored
In the quiet harbour
Wild ! Untamed !
Or ...
My arms have opened wide
To spread around the gnarled
And knotted trunk
Of such an old, old tree !
There to sense the stream of 'life'
In continuity !
Such beauty there !
For me.

17. *Your Beautiful World (5)*

Your world is so beautiful—it hurts me !
I looked at daffodils today
The colour ... lovely, singing colour
It took my breath away ... nearly !
Then ...
I watched the clear stream water trickle over pebbles—
Saw the patterns in them, clear and bright
Not one was like the other
In your beautiful world.
I saw ...
The silver sheen of water
Like a sheet of glass, so still,
At rest between quiet hills
Reflecting the grey of the sky.
And, mirrored there,
A bird,
Motionless, hovering for a moment
Then, wheeling and turning,
It had gone
On its way,
In Your beautiful world !

II

You and Your Church

I'm looking for You
Everywhere!
Sometimes, just for a moment,
I think I've found You!
Then again . . .
There are times when I know
I can never exhaust the possibilities
Of knowing You!

It's exciting, isn't it?
(Is that really what You had in mind?)

1. Other Christians

I guess You're going to find this hard to believe.
I really don't quite know how to say it,
But . . .
I get along just fine with folks
Who don't profess anything at all!
It's those who are supposed to be Christian
That I have problems with!
I wonder if they realize that other people
Are sometimes nicer to be with
Than they are?
But . . . it's true, You know!

Do You think they sometimes forget
To try . . . to make efforts to be nice?
Why don't they make an effort
To be interesting?
I'm quite sure You don't really want to be represented
By people who seem dull and boring,
And whose horizons in life are so narrow.

Yes! I suppose I am going on a bit,
But, You must confess that it's sometimes so true!
(Oh . . . You do, but . . . not always in the third person!)
OK. Message received and understood!
It's 'we' and not 'they' . . . I suppose!
Yes . . . I know that it's sometimes difficult
To see the good inside the family—
But, You did agree—
There is something in what I say!

2. Dear Souls

Today
I met one of your 'dear souls' —
At least, that's what my Mum would call her.
And, somehow, it suited her.
Sheer goodness just seemed to ooze from her.
You couldn't pin it down
You just recognized it, somehow!

I wasn't with her long
But
She did me good!
I think she'd probably be surprised
If she knew.

I would like to be like that!
Is it possible, when you're young?
Or is it something
That seems to happen to you
When you are older?

Anyway...
Thanks for letting my life touch hers.

3. 'Gloom' Day

It's 'gloom' day today!
Sorry about that, but we can't help it.
We've just been told
A new club leader has been appointed
And, honestly . . .
We just don't know what to do about it!

He's what my Dad would call,
'A very worthy young man',
And we've nothing against him at all—
Except as the leader of the Club!
It's just not on!

We heard that he volunteered
And I do wish they would watch that kind of thing!
Just because a person volunteers
It doesn't mean they're always suitable,
Does it?
And . . . boy . . . he isn't!

(What's that?)

O yes, of course . . . we'll give him a chance.
I mean . . . you can't do anything else, can you?
But I just hope that he'll have enough sense
To get the message!

4. Love . . . In quotes

I think I'd better warn You,
I'm pretty wound-up.
(Do I ever wind-down? . . . Yes, that's a good question!)
But, honestly, it makes me sick!
There they all are
Sitting up there; all in place
Wearing holy expressions;
Looking 'pi'!
Making all the conventional noises.

Well, it won't wash . . . I'm sorry!
It just won't!
And, what's more, I don't think it really impresses anyone—
Certainly not me!
Well, frankly . . . if You'd been with me
In the committee and heard them
Tearing people to shreds.
People who have helped me . . . terrifically!
People who have got more caring and compassion
In their little fingers
Than that lot have got in the whole of their
Self righteous bodies!
(Oh, yes, of course! You were there!
And You did hear!
Gosh, they'd have a shock, if they remembered that,
    wouldn't they?)

5. Why?

Can You tell me something?
It's something that's been on my mind for some time
Now!
It puzzles me,
I just don't understand.
Here we are, all the time, listening to sermons,
Preaching about it,
Discussing it!
This 'loving our neighbour as ourselves' bit.
Yet at the drop of a hat
We're at each other! Tooth and nail,
No holds barred!
I just don't get it. Do You?
When someone steps out of line
Why isn't the first thought . . .
'How can we try to understand this?' Or . . .
'Let's try to see his point of view.' Or . . .
'Well he's certainly made a bad mistake.
What can we do to lighten the disaster for him?'

But it isn't . . . is it? Often!
And I don't think we should kid ourselves about it.
Do You?
(No . . . I thought You wouldn't!)

6. Your Church

People don't like Your Church, You know!
It's a non-starter with some folk!
(Oh . . . it's no reflection on You, mind!)
But, somehow, they just don't seem to take to it.
It doesn't click with them, does it?

Where have we gone wrong,
Because it must be us . . . mustn't it?
(Oh . . . not always? How come, then?)
Oh . . . I see, they have a responsibility too!
Well, that's encouraging.
I felt sure it was bound to be us, again!

Seriously, though . . .
I am concerned!
I do want to represent You as well as I can . . .
And most people
Just couldn't care less!

Is it because sometimes it's hard to be a Christian,
And stick to ideas of decency and integrity
And goodness?
I don't mind so much, if that's it.
I just couldn't bear it
If it was because we're stuffy and narrow-minded
And turned in on ourselves.
It isn't that . . . is it?

7. Snobs

Oh they are a load of snobs
And it does upset me !
I've really had enough !
And for once, my Mum and Dad say I'm right . . .
(And that's a turn up for the book) !
But it doesn't make me feel any better.

All right . . . so . . . those two sisters
Aren't very with it, or well turned-out !
Maybe they'll never look like swingers.
So what !
In heaven's name . . . is that so very vital?
With their home background
It's a miracle they're even with us !

Anyway, you'd think they'd got the measles
To see the careful way our lot avoid them . . .
(Oh yes . . . the same lot that sing
'When I needed a neighbour, were you there?')
That's them, all right !

Ooooooo . . . I'm so cross
It's coming out of my ears !
Do calm me down, or else I'm going to say something
I'll be sorry for . . .
And You won't like very much . . . either !

8. Involvement

Some people do make me annoyed!
Honestly . . . I get so mad.
For instance, there was this man on the radio
This morning.
He was going on about the Church being removed
From where people are.
Not being involved with life.
Well, really!
I nearly rang the BBC and said . . .
'This is the Church, right on the end of your phone!'
After all, the Church isn't some abstract affair!
It's me, all seventeen years of me . . .
And lots of others like me.
And we're not removed, are we?
I get the bus to the station and catch the 8.15 every morning,
And so do about two million others (all on my train—
Or so it seems, sometimes!)
I don't see how you can be more involved with life
Than that!
There they are . . . reading their newspapers,
Chatting about this and that; and there am I,
Doing the same
I don't work on my own, either. They're there too . . .
Tapping the other typewriters . . .
Making the tea, and drinking it with me!
They're there . . . all . . . day.

And if I go out at night, even to the Wimpy Bar . . .
There they all are again . . . eating double egg and chips,
Just like me!

OK . . . I am calming down . . .
But it made me see red.
It seems to me some people think the Church is just
Made up of ministers and services and things like that.
They forget that it's me . . .
And lots of others like me,
Living in the world,
Doing all kinds of things that everyone else does—
But with a difference . . .
Consciously linked in with You!
And trying to work out Your great ideas
Here in the strait-jacket of human nature.

Well! If You want to know what I think,
Here it is . . . for free!
I sometimes think we're a bloomin' miracle!

9. *Inspiration*

I'd like a word with You
About Your Church.
(All right, perhaps it is mine as well.
At least, I'm part of it.)
Well, then . . . isn't it time
You inspired us to something new and fresh . . .
Something world-shattering?

Everything we do seems to be old-hat and stale
These days.
You must be quite disappointed, really.
I mean to say, it was such a great idea
In the beginning, wasn't it?
With folk dying for their faith,
Whole governments being converted,
And the world turned up-side-down?

Why did I have to live now, and not then;
Now, when the church idea seems stale and jaded.

Yes, I know I'm young, and it's easy to talk.
But isn't it important to feel like this now?
It seems to me folk don't gain in enthusiasm
As they get older!

10. Feeling and Faith

Today is a day
When it's difficult for me
To feel anything about You . . . at all !
I get days like this, don't I ?
That doesn't mean You're not there tho',
Does it ?
Someone said, the other day,
That it was like a TV set
Not turned on.
The programmes are all happening—
But you've got to tune in,
Switch on, to experience them.
Because I'm not watching
It doesn't mean they've ceased to happen !
Don't You think faith is a bit like a radar system ?
You really know it's working but you can't see a thing !
Yet you know exactly where you are.

It's a bit like that with You and me . . . isn't it ?
Sometimes I can't feel a thing
Yet I know exactly where I am . . .
And I know that . . . You . . . are !

11. God Is . . . (1)

Knowing You . . .
Is like moving through the score
Of a mighty symphony!

A soft gentle melody
That lingers on its own —
Is joined by richest harmonies
That sweep it onwards
In rich, turbulent sound;
Majestic, sonorous, soaring and sweeping
To a mighty climax point —
And sudden silence!
A solo instrument takes up the theme again
In minor mood and unaccompanied . . .
It cries alone.
Then, note by note, the richness is returning . . .
Till at its height
It sings a deathless song
That mounts into the sky.

This cosmic theme
Is sounding thro' my life.
If I but add my voice
We shall make harmony, together!

12. God Is . . . (2)

Knowing You . . .
Is like having a great, glowing jewel
Suspended in the centre of my life —
Turning, slowly.
Is it blue?
No, green . . . but, surely,
Here and there, a brilliant flash of ruby?
Streaked with gold, and yet not gold, but
Turning now to amber, orange, flame . . .
Down, down again, to purest white
Then silver!

You are so many colours to me,
And in the mirror of my life
Each one strikes its own
Peculiar beauty.

13. God Is . . . (3)

Knowing You is like an eternal voyage of discovery!
You are like a great big, uncharted continent ...
I sail my boat and touch but the fringe,
Just the shore line.
And even this seems to stretch into infinity ...
Set against a backdrop of long plateaux
Moving back to endless hills
Giving way to towering mountains
Seemingly impenetrable—
And yet ...
I can go there—I know I can!

All I have to do is beach my boat on the shore—
And You are there
For me!

14. Jesus

Do You know that some folk understand You best
When they contemplate the universe—
Watch the moving patterns of stars and planets—
And the ceaseless ebb and flow of the sun and moon
Along the cosmic trails?
  And sometimes, I do, too!

Then there are those, who, feeling the mighty
Throbbing pulse of Beethoven, the lilting strains of
Schubert, say ' I sense God here.'
  And I do, too . . .

To touch the satin petal of a buttercup in June,
And feel the gentle breeze that plays among the apple trees.
Or walk along the wide sea-shore in mounting gale . . .
Is to know that this is You . . .
  And I know, too!

But when I want to know that You understand my feelings,
And when I must be sure there is Someone there who cares,
And when I feel alone and frightened into silence . . .
Not even very sure if there are answers to my prayers.

  Then I look at Jesus
  And gradually I see,
  A perfect-formed reflection
  Of what You are . . . for me!

15. Representing God (1)

Ooooooooooo . . . some people do get under my skin!
I'm sorry, but it's true.
This week, at school, it's been murder! Honestly!
Some folk seem to think that if you say you are a Christian
Then it means you are some kind of miracle—
And I'm not!

There's one fellow who I'm sure waits around for me
Then, if I dare put a foot wrong—
It doesn't need to be much—
Just a snappy remark—a back answer—
A hot-headed opinion—
And he's at you!
'Oh fancy . . .' he'll drawl, 'I thought Christians were
    supposed
To turn the other cheek!'
Or: 'Well, well, well . . . where's the "meek and lowly"
    business
Now, then?'

Honestly . . . it makes you sick!
The trouble is, I don't know what to do.
I want to try to be myself,
Not some holier-than-thou type—
And yet, he doesn't give me a chance!
He makes me feel as if I shouldn't have any faults and
    failings—
And I know that's not possible . . . is it?
Oh . . . do help me stick it out—
I'd hate him to think he'd
Sunk my ship!

16. Representing God (2)

Can I come back on that?
You see,
The trouble is I'm worried
In case he gets turned off Christianity
Because of me!
Do You think that is possible?
But then again—to be perfectly honest—
He's going to find that all the other Christian guys
Are much the same, isn't he?
(I hoped You'd agree on that one!)

So, what's to be done?
Just stick it out? Is that the tactic?
Keep on plugging away?
Well, I just hope You will be
So strong a holding factor in me,
That I'll manage not to lose my temper with him—
I've a feeling that would put the fat in the fire!
So, I'm relying on You!

17. A Better Moment

I suppose this is one of what you might call
My better moments!
I do have them occasionally ...
Yes, it is surprising —
But sitting here, in the quiet of myself, the real me —
Somehow, I am experiencing You.
I don't know You as the textbook God
Some of them make You out to be!
Somehow You've never taken on that kind of shape or feel
For me!
That's the problem, really!
They expect me to be able to talk about You
Like they do;
But for me, that's like trying to dam up the oceans
Or trap a star in its cosmic bed;
So ... I don't!
But now, suddenly, in this quiet moment
You are!
And I know that You are!
Just live and grow in me, please!
And help me remember ... now!

18. Reminding Things

I saw the morning sunlight
Slanting through the trees in our road
              And I thought of You!

There were two kids,
Holding hands on the train; 'in love';
              And I thought of You!

A dog ran up and licked my hand,
For no reason at all;
He had lovely eyes,
              And I thought of You!

I saw a funeral going by ... slowly!
I felt sorry for them
              And I thought of You!

I got into bed, last night ... Feeling grateful
For everything; my home, my work, my friends,
And my loved ones :
              And I thought of You!

Thanks for reminding things!

19. An Understanding Moment

Do You know
Just sometimes
I can understand why the people in the Bible
Spoke to You in such solemn and grand language!
It must have been because—sometimes,
Just sometimes—
You seem to be that kind of God!

Take today, for instance,
I sat in church
And heard an organ playing
And the music seemed to fill my life
With Your presence!

III

Me — and My Relationships

I could manage fine, You know,
If it were not for other people!
(Yes, I know . . . that's the catch,
Isn't it?)
Never mind,
So long as I can depend on You to understand—
Then I'm ready for them all!
(Only, don't go away,
Will You?)

1. Disliking Someone

If You like, I'll pretend,
And make excuses and defend myself!
But the truth of the matter is that
I don't like him very much.
In fact, I don't like him
At all.
I can't stick him.
There . . .
Somehow it helps to get it off my chest
To You.
Oh, I know You know all about it anyway—
But not from me;
And that's important.

Do you think You can help in this?
Is there a chance that You, in me,
Can like him so much
That eventually he'll become tolerable to me?

I'll give You a chance, shall I?
Have a go . . .
I promise I'll try not to get in the way.

2. A Discovery (about not liking people)

You know, it's sickeningly true.
I've tried to persuade myself
That it would work out differently—
But I'm being forced to realize
That there are people
I am just never going to be able to like!

I know I've told You about this before
And before
And before that, too!
But, You see, *then* I thought that if I worked at it
It might be different
But it isn't ... really!

Dad says that this is what loving is all about:
Not just liking the folk you get on with well,
Who 'tick' like you do
(If You know what I mean),
But cultivating (that's a good word, isn't it?)
An active attitude of goodwill towards those you don't
Get on with!
(That sounds like my Dad, doesn't it?)

Oh, I know he's right ... yes!
The trouble is ... doing it.
It ... is ... such ... hard ... work!
It wears you out, literally!
If it weren't for You, in me, helping—
I think I'd have given up, long ago!

Oh, I see ! That's the idea, is it?
Well, let me tell You this—
It's no 'picnic' allowing You to use me for this
Loving business !
Sometimes it feels as tho' I'm being torn apart ...

3. *About Loving*

I'm back again about that 'loving' business!
I'm sorry to bore You with it again,
But what's really bugging me is this—
The more I push my own reactions to the back
And let You, in me, react to the folk I don't like,
The worse they seem to become!
Don't they have any obligation in this thing, as well?

(They do? . . . but it's none of my business!)
Well, OK, I accept that.
But I wish I could see that they were aware of it—*too*!
(That's nothing to do with me, either!)
Oh . . . I see! I'm just the one who has to work at this
    business
Of allowing You so much in my life
That . . . gradually it won't irritate so much?
Oh . . . come on now! It can't be that one-sided!
(It is?)
Well, that's that then! Isn't it? I mean . . .
I've got it straight, haven't I?
But frankly, if I may say so,
I don't think You've half an idea
Of what it's like sometimes!

(You do, You have, and You did it all Yourself?)
Yes.
I've a habit of forgetting that,
Haven't I?

4. The 'Clingy' Types

Look ...
I'd like to make this clear, from the start!
I don't want to be unkind—really, I don't,
But this isn't a friendship.
This is a propping-up society!

What can I do about it?
He's invading my life, taking over—almost!
I just haven't got that kind of time.
And I haven't got that kind of energy—
Well, at least not non-stop!

I don't think he's got a clue what real friendship
Is all about.
You know ... the give and take,
And the sharing!
With him—it's all take ... take ... take!
(SILENCE)

I'm sorry—yes, I am a bit 'het-up',
But ... I think the problem is
I don't know what to do!
We've talked about it, at home,
And they understand that he really needs friendship.
But even Dad's getting a bit edgy about him always being
    there!
But ... what to do?
I can't just abruptly tell him to stop coming around
Each evening, can I?
But even if I say I'm going out
He suggests coming too!

You really can't win !
(SILENCE)

Yes, You're right . . .
I am a bit of a coward !
I really don't want to have to say it . . . straight out !
I was hoping he'd take hints.
But even if I spelt it out in neon signs,
I think he'd miss it !
And it's not only that—
I really would be quite happy to have him as
One of my friends,
But not the only one !
I'm sure he'll never understand that,
In a 'month of Sundays'.

I've tried trying to link him with the others—
But they think he's such a drag,
And he is . . . sometimes !
(I think even You would have to admit that !)

Actually, what I do want You to know is . . .
That I've decided to be out tomorrow night when he comes.
And now I've done it
I feel bad !
(Yes, I know that I've got to face it out, sometime !
But it doesn't feel good !)
(SILENCE)

(You think it may help him to learn he can't
    monopolize my time ? . . .
Only I must be careful not to become blasé about it,
And not make any attempt to help him through this
Period of readjustment ! Oh, thanks ! That helps me to
    know !)
That's fair ! I accept that and I'll try !
Could You please help him to begin to understand
And accept it ?

5. First Love — from her point of view

It happened tonight . . .
We walked up through the trees, and suddenly—
He kissed me!
(Are You interested in this?)
Everything seemed to burst around me—
All stars and things!
It sounds silly really, but it wasn't at the time—
It was lovely; I think!
Only, I don't know what it means . . .

I lay in bed and thought about it . . . and him!
Is this what they call love?
How long will I feel like this?
There seemed to be a queue of questions . . .
And I could still feel the nearness of him!
Lovely . . . !

I want this to be a good thing—
Help me not to read too much, or too little
Into it—
But help me not to turn away from it . . .
Because I'm scared,
                or embarrassed,
                        or unwilling to share myself!
It's not easy, You know!

6. *First Love — from his point of view*

It happened tonight . . .
We walked up through the trees, and suddenly—
I couldn't help it—
I kissed her !

Her great eyes looked at me, and I thought—
'Oh heck ! What have I done !'
Being with her has been great,
I don't want to spoil it !
What if she didn't like it ?
Or thought I'd got a nerve ?
(I hope You're going to help !)

I've a feeling it's all right, though ;
Do You know what I mean ?
Because I held her hand as we walked on—
And I think she was smiling . . .

Help me, please !
Don't let it all get too much for me !

7. Parents' Understanding

No one understands ... You know!
Just no one!
They've all forgotten what it's like to be young.
They feel as though they're a hundred and ninety, at least—
The way they talk!
You'd think I was asking for the crown jewels
And not just to come home by eleven o'clock—
I ask you—eleven o'clock!
What's so outrageous about that?
And yet there's my Mum with a face like the crack of doom;
And Dad popping anxious looks around the newspaper
As though he expects to see 'Juvenile Delinquent'
Appear like a neon sign above my head ...
I give up!
But, I thought You'd like to know.
Not that I expect any help from You.
I know what You'll say ...
That they're only worried because they love me;
That I ought to try to see it their way too,
And co-operate ...
Well OK ... but I tell You this,
They're enough to try the patience of a saint sometimes!

OK, OK, so—I know I'm no saint!

8. Cliques

What do You think about cliques?
We've just been given a blast
By Jean's Dad about leaving her out!
Rita stuttered something about not really meaning it . . .
Not thinking about it . . . and all that.
I just stood!
I felt awful.
I wanted to shout— 'But you don't really know her,
                She's a drag, a bore
                She doesn't even try to be with it
                And interesting.
                It's her own fault!'
And, the worst thing about it is,
It would all have been true!
I didn't say it, of course,
Well, you can't, can you?

(What do You mean . . . why?)
Well, yes, I suppose You're right,
I did think it!
But to come back to cliques.
Don't You think she ought to at least make some effort?
(You do?) Well, good!
(But so should we?) OK. Fair 'do's', I suppose!
I wish I could work up some enthusiasm for it.
(You'll help?) Well, thanks a lot!
I'll hold You to that!

9. Being Dropped — (from her angle)

I don't really know what to say to You about this.
It's a really grotty feeling;
You see . . . it was such a shock!
We were just walking home together
And suddenly he said—
'Don't you think we're getting a little serious
About each other? I think we should cool it a bit,
See something of other folk—after all, we're a bit young
To be getting so involved, aren't we?'
I realized, then, just how much I liked him
And how wrapped up in him I had become!

Well, of course, I said 'yes'—
I mean . . . what else could I say?
But I felt quite sick!
The worst of it was, I kept wishing I'd said it first!
(My Mum would say that just goes to show it's my pride
    that's hurt
And not my feelings.)
Not that she knows about it, of course!
In fact, nobody does . . . except You!
I just can't seem to say it—out aloud.
It's awful! I keep pretending things are just the same,
And people are going to expect that it is so.
What's really getting me is trying to behave as if I don't
    care—
Because I do!

I know that I ought to be calm and dignified,
Sensible, and tell people quietly
That we're not quite as friendly as we were—
That's what he is doing;
But it's all right for him
He wants it that way!
But, honestly, I can't tell anyone else this—
I wish we were back, just as we always were!
Is that so terrible?

I hope You understand—
Because, somehow,
You are going to have to help me through this!
I know, deep down inside
That it's not the end of the world—
But I do miss him,
And the things we shared together.
And I miss being 'special' for someone.
I'm glad I can share it with You
Because I'll never be able to tell Mum!

10. Being Dropped — (from his angle)

I just wish she'd told me ... that's all.
I mean, even You must agree
If you've had a good friendship
You ought to be able to tell each other things!
Even difficult things—
Or is that just what the textbooks say
And it never really happens!

I suppose I ought to have guessed
That she was cooling off—
She must have put on a jolly good act;
Either that, or I'm particularly thick!
Anyway—I didn't know—
And that's all there is to it!

The worst thing is that
I've a feeling she has discussed it all with her best friend—
And I can't stick the thought of that.
It makes me want to go out and
Find myself another girl—sharpish—
Just to show I can ... I suppose!
(Yes, I agree ... that cheapens the whole thing!)

Help me to get a grip on myself, please!
I've got to see it in perspective, haven't I?
It's not the end of the world—
It just feels like it, at the moment!

11. The Wrong Boy-Friend

I've done it again . . .
Honestly, my Dad says I've got a heart like an hotel,
And I'm inclined to think he's right!
I just couldn't say 'no' when he asked me out,
He looked so anxious, and he is a bit dishy,
After all!
But, it won't work, You know—
(You do know . . . don't *You*?)
We're as different as chalk from cheese, really!
And, boy! does it show!
We haven't a single thing to talk about!
We nattered on about the meal, the décor
And the weather—a film or two . . .
I was glad when the coffee came.

What am I going to do?
Mum says I've to tell him, straight out—
It's all right for her, she hasn't got to do it!
I don't want to hurt him,
That's not fair, is it?
But it's not fair to let him think everything's OK,
Is it?
Oh heck! I wish I wasn't a girl!
(No . . . You're right . . . I don't mean that . . .)
I just mean I wish I didn't get into such stupid situations!

Please, at least help me not to be a coward
When I tell him . . .
Help me to stick by what I say!

72

12. The Wrong Girl-Friend

I could see it in their faces,
The minute I introduced her!
They were surprised ... and I suppose, if I'm honest
I knew they would be.
She is a bit way-out
And she doesn't really bother to put on the old charm bit.
Mum was worried; I could see all the symptoms.
She kept touching her hair and moving the cushions
And pushing the conversation along!
When I came back, after taking her home,
Mum was still up, and I thought
'Here it comes' ... but it didn't.
She didn't say anything ... and that was worse, somehow;
Because if she'd liked her
She'd have chattered non-stop.
You'd have almost heard the wedding bells!

I know they won't say anything to me.
You know, don't You, that they believe in me
Making my own decisions?
Only this time I can't seem to sort it out!
I can't just drop her flat! (You wouldn't expect that,
Would You?)
On the other hand,
I just know it won't work out!
Either way, she's going to think I'm some sort of monster,
Isn't she?
(Stay alongside for a bit, will You?
I could use some help!)

13. Casual Attitudes

I've discovered something
That can make my blood boil—
(No, I don't suppose that comes as any great shock
    to You, come to think of it!)
But, seriously,
I don't like being taken for granted.
I don't like it being assumed
That I will go . . . or come . . . or react in any way!
(Mum says that it sounds like
    the 'pot calling the kettle black' to her!)
Well . . . maybe it's a bit true
That I can do a bit of it myself!
But I'll make jolly sure that I don't . . . in the future.
After all, people are people!
They're not puppets . . . or robots . . .
They have feelings, reactions, and their own point of view.
And . . . so do I!
I'm . . . me!
(SILENCE)

Good heavens! I don't believe it!
I'm actually right, am I
For once?

14. Family Love

I had a shock today!
It was unexpected too!
(Well, I suppose shocks usually are, aren't they?)
I went home for tea with Catherine.
And that's all there is to it ... really!
Except that it wasn't what I would have called 'home'!
I won't go into details
Because it isn't fair really!
I suppose I'm just lucky, aren't I?
My Mum and Dad may get on to us a bit,
But it's only because they care about us, isn't it?

It was a relief to get home.
I walked in (banging the door as usual),
Dad was measuring up some new cupboards for Mum;
Our kid was lying on the floor
Watching the telly
(When he should have been doing his homework!);
Mum was baking and looked all hot and floury,
And she nearly had a fit when I walked in,
Put my arms round her, and kissed her!
But, it was all so blessedly normal
And home-like!

No way-out décor!
No smart new Mum!
No smart Alec Dad, trying to chat-up the visitor,
Just us ...
And I do love the way we are!

IV

Me – and My Responsibilities

It would be easier not to face up to them,
To pretend they are not there !
(But anyway, You wouldn't let me
Get away with that, would You?)
So, I'm having a go !
That's all You really ask of me,
Isn't it?

1. Exaggerating

Do You know? I don't even notice I'm doing it!
It was such a shock when my friend picked me up on it
The other day.
Such a simple thing:
I was telling someone how long we had waited for the bus.
Actually it was ten minutes, and I said—
'I had to wait nearly twenty minutes for a bus!'
Of course, I didn't mean it
But it wasn't quite truthful, I suppose, even so!

I guess I'll have to watch it, and I'd like Your help.
You see, I've a feeling it could become a habit;
And that one day it might be important that my word
    could be depended upon.
Actually I'm at my worst when I'm spinning a yarn—
I stretch it sometimes almost beyond believing—
OK, so . . .
I know it's not quite what You would call a sin,
But it's certainly getting to be a habit
And I don't want to become a person nobody believes
Any more.
I know someone like that, or rather, to be accurate,
Dad does.
He says this man, and what he says, really doesn't count
    any more!

Is it possible to give me a nudge, every so often?
I'd appreciate that!

79

2. Example

Boy!
Something happened this morning
That really set me back on my heels.
I was trying to rush-finish my maths homework.
Mum was fussing about eating breakfast—
Dad was carrying on about the fact that
I should have done it last night, etc. etc.
When my married sister's three-year-old
(He's staying with us for a week)
Knocked his glass of milk all over my maths homework!
I let out a few choice words!
Mum came to the rescue, mopped him and me up—
Calmed me down,
Settled him with some bricks,
And calm prevailed . . .
Only . . .
Not quite!
Above the murmur of Radio 2
I heard, quite clearly, my young nephew
Saying those choice words,
Over, and over and over . . . again!
I thought Dad's eyebrows would never come down again—
And Mum's look was a study!

Well, I just want You to know
I got the message!
No . . . more than that—
I'm dreadfully sorry about it all!
I think it was worse because
Nobody said anything to me!
Perhaps they guessed how ghastly I felt!

3. Not Realizing

Woweeeeee . . .
What a day !
I think You're the only one left
Who isn't mad at me !
Mum's upset, and Dad's had a go at me
For upsetting Mum . . . and that's how it is !
I just can't win.
I feel a bit battered, actually—
I didn't mean to be awkward
It's just that different things are important
To different people—isn't it?
And I didn't realise that being there, last night,
Was important for them.
So, I fixed to go out !

Yes, I know I should have checked about it
But I didn't,
Did I?

Yes, I've made a mental note of it—
And it won't happen again . . .
But I really could use Your help
To soften up the atmosphere a bit !

4. Hurting People (1)

It's no good.
I've just got to get this one off my chest!
I can't settle to work,
I can't forget her face . . .
We shouldn't have said what we did!
Oh, I know she had to know—sometime,
But, it wasn't the right moment,
And it wasn't the right place!
We didn't help her,
We just hurt her . . .
And really, that's unforgiveable, isn't it?

We could have avoided it, You know—
We could!
One of us should have had the guts
To tell her personally, and privately,
But we were all chicken!
That's what it amounts to, isn't it?
We just queued up to hide behind each other!
And I shouldn't be saying 'we', should I?
It should be 'I' . . .
(Yes, You thought I'd never get round to that,
Didn't You?)

Well, I just hope You're going to help me
Get around there,
And say that, I, for one, am sorry for it all!

Serves me right if she won't open the door!

5. Hurting People (2)

It's still no good, You know . . .
It just isn't !
I've been round, Bill has, and even Jim . . .
But it's not right !
Oh, she's very pleasant—frankly I think she's a bloomin'
    saint
About it; but it isn't the same.
I've a horrible feeling
It isn't ever going to be the same again.

Why don't people tell you that?
When they say—like Dad did, for instance—
'Get round there and put it right !'
You can 'put it right' as much as you like
But really, the damage is done;
And just because you feel all sorry
And full of the best of intentions
To make up for it . . .
It doesn't mean she isn't hurt any more
Because she is !

You've just got to think before you act,
Haven't you?
That's the important thing ! Don't say it !
Well, I've learned my lesson.
Do You think You could help?
You know—make her feel less hurt, please?
We seem to have gummed up the situation,
Completely . . . between us !

6. Choice

Soon ... I've got to decide!
It's inevitable
I can't dodge it!
(Yes! You're right—I have tried to—
But it all misfired
And, I'm back where I started.)
I've got to decide.

I'd like You to know there are times,
Just occasionally,
When I'd rather we didn't have free-will;
When I almost wish life were pre-recorded!
(Do You know what I mean?)
The effort of trying to weigh up,
Assess, strip the problem down to its basics!
It all becomes too much!

All I really want to be sure of ...
Is that I'm choosing the right things!
The things You can be in.
Please invade my thinking
And set me on the right course!
Please!

7. Stocktaking Myself (over the typewriter)

Well . . . I didn't exactly cover myself in glory there,
Did I?
But, there's a limit to what you can take, You know . . .
Yes . . . I know I shouldn't have allowed myself to be
    drawn—
I knew they were getting at me . . .
But I couldn't help it !
I'm not 'pi' and stuffy, and Victorian,
I'm sick of being thought of like that !
I'm just normal . . . aren't I ?
I mean . . . I like boys, and nice clothes,
And being taken out
Just as much as any of them !
But I honestly don't think that's all there is
To life !
They do . . . You know !
And what's more—it's true—
I am sick of hearing all the finer details of
What happened with their boy friends last night,
And the endless comparisons—one with another !
It's cheap . . . It makes them sound like things
And not people !
(Yes ! I know I'm worked up about it . . . But
I feel strongly about it ! OK, I'll simmer down,
But it doesn't mean I feel any the less deeply !)

Well, the top-and-bottom of it is . . .
What am I going to do?
Was it wrong to say what I did?
(It wasn't! Oh, good! At least I did something right!)
But it wasn't the best way to say it the way I did . . .
Is that what you mean? Well then—
I'll have to watch that, won't I?
Can't have them thinking I'm an old 'grumpy-dick'
Or they won't get a very good impression of Christians,
Will they?

8. Give Me a Hand!

I'm going to have to watch myself.
Give me a Hand, please!
My Mum's quite right—money slips through my fingers
Like water—
And it's not really very Christian to be careless—is it?
It's just that I honestly didn't think about it!
Until I sat right down and totted up what I'd spent
On myself—during the last month!
No wonder I had to borrow two quid off my Mum
For the Oxfam appeal!

Two quid . . .
The price of four 'singles'.
(OK, OK, and the price of keeping four children in rice
    for a month . . . I know! Don't rub it in!)
It's a bit shattering though!

I'm going to need a hand to keep this in the front of my
    mind,
It's there . . .
But somehow it slips to the back
And it's forgotten again.

Give me a Hand, please!

9. A First Job

It's really been an eye opener
Since I've been working for my living!
I've never had to be constantly with the same people
For so long, each day.
People tend to get on each other's nerves,
Don't they?
And, of course, you can't get away, can you?
You have to stay and be with them.

Actually, I'm finding quite a lot of things
A bit heavy going!
I want to keep moving round,
Instead of staying at my desk.
I want to chat, too —
And you can imagine how that's received!
I'm terribly tired, too,
At the end of the day —
Whereas they all seem to come to life at 5.30 p.m.,
All rarin' to go!
I suppose they're used to it all!

I don't like to let on at home about it;
It's not bad, really —
And I know they're all dying for me to do well!
I don't want them to worry
Or feel disappointed —
So, I'm telling You again.
Help me, please!
Help me get used to an ordered routine —
To work at appreciating the folk who work with me —
To adjust to the whole idea of . . . work!

10. Saying What You Mean

There was a row in the office today—
I knew it had been warming-up to this for some time,
But I was surprised when it happened.
Well . . . it was such a little thing, really!
But it made me think!

Do You think it is right always to say what you feel?
For instance—if you are asked for an opinion,
And you know what you are going to say
Is not what the person really wants to hear;
Should you still say it and be honest?
Or is it kinder either to pretend you don't have an opinion,
Or say something completely evasive
That lets you out?
Isn't it difficult—this conflict between
Kindness and honesty?

And here's another thing!
How much depends on the way you say something?
You know—the tone of voice,
The expression on your face, and so forth—
I'm beginning to think life would be so much easier
If we didn't say anything at all!
It's certainly true for the office—today,
And it worries me!

11. Thank You For The World

Today I feel ashamed—
Ashamed of all the moaning, complaining,
Criticizing and fault-finding
That I am capable of . . .

It happened like this—
I watched some tiny children
In a school for the disabled
Make their slow, painful way to the dinner table
Helped by calipers, walking frames,
Wheelchairs . . .
It took quite some time to get them settled.
Suddenly their infant voices were raised in song—
      'Thank you for the world so sweet,
      Thank you for the food we eat,
      Thank you for the birds that sing—
      Thank you God . . . for *everything*!'

O God . . . please take this strong feeling of mine now
And remind me of it when I'm tempted to be ungrateful;
Because just now—I feel
I shall never have the right to complain again.

12. Getting on People's Nerves

I just know that I'm getting on everyone's nerves, today!
I can feel it!
I'm too loud,
Talking too much,
Laughing too much,
Butting in—offering opinions where they're not wanted—
Putting my foot in it,
Left, right and centre!

I just can't seem to stop!
I feel full of it!
Full of life, of fun, of movement,
Of expression!
Anything but work (as my long-suffering colleagues
Have just pointed out)!

Can You help me contain it?
I just must not let my energies spill out
And upset and dislocate everyone else's day,
Must I?

I guess this is what Mum would call
Discipline, isn't it?

13. Discriminating

I say . . . what do You think?
Mum's just given me a pat on the back!
She says—just listen to this—she says
That I'm learning to discriminate!
How about that?
And all because I said I was going out with Jim
And not Pete, tonight.
You see, Jim's kind of quiet and a bit shy,
Whereas Pete's quite a bobby-dazzler!
(She worries about the bobby-dazzlers. You know!)
Anyway, I'm basking in her approval,
While I've got it.

In a way, I think she's got a point, actually.
I think I am learning a thing or two.
After all, what's the use of being all swoony
Over the way he looks,
If you can't find anything to talk about?
There's a lot more to people than
The way they look—
Isn't there?

14. Making Time

I do hate being behind
All the time !

Yes, I know it's my own fault
I ought to pull my socks up
And get on with things !
But somehow there's always something else to do !

I'm going to make a real effort ...
Next week !

Yes — I know I've said it before,
But this time I mean it !
Really I do !

I'm so glad we know each other,
You know !
You'd never believe anything I said, otherwise —
Would You?

15. Making Efforts

I've had a bad day—today.
Somehow nothing's clicked!
Honestly, by dinnertime, I was all for giving up,
Going home and calling it a day.
Nobody will ever know what it cost me
Just to stay put . . .
Never mind getting on with my work—
Just to stay . . .

I suppose that's really what's bugging me.
There was I,
Stoically sitting it out—
At heaven knows what cost—
And no one even noticed.

I know what You'll say!
That that's what it's all about;
Life . . . I mean!
Getting quietly on with growing-up
Maturing, becoming a person
Even when nobody notices!

OK . . . so—
I just hope You know
It's almost too much for me—
Sometimes!

94

V

Me — and My Reactions

The trouble with me is
I'm my own worst enemy!
You really are going to have a job
With me!
But . . . if You're ready for it—
So am I!
(I nearly said 'Let battle commence'—
Well it may turn out to be like that
In spite of my good intentions.)

1. Out of Proportion

I could kick myself!
Honestly!
I must have taken leave of my senses—or something!
Well, whatever happened,
I got the whole thing completely out of proportion.
(Dad says it's typical of females—
Mum overheard! Exit Dad!)
I feel so silly . . . so terribly silly!
And I know I made myself look a fool
In front of the kids at the club.
So now,
It's difficult to know how to . . . be!
(Dad says . . . 'Forget it!'
Mum says I ought to apologize quietly!)

So . . . what do *You* say?

Give it some thought . . . and wait?
All right—
I'll try and ride out this one more easily
With *Your* help.

2. A Safety Valve

Poor old Jim!
He's just had to take the lot . . . again!
I'd bottled it up all the evening
And the minute we got outside
Wooooosh! Out it came!

He really is a love!
Not many fellows would sit it out like he does.
He just turned the car ignition off —
Settled back in his seat, and said,
'Right-o, luv, rattle away,
And get it off your chest.' And I did!

Well, I think he knew just as well as I did
That the whole evening had been a waste of time!
(And he's doing his finals, too.
He really needs time for study!)
We had just rambled on and on . . . around the point
Under it, above it . . . anywhere but on it!
And I say
You can't expect people to turn up to committee meetings
If they're run that way . . . well—can you?

Anyway, bless his heart
I poured it all out . . . and he listened!

Many thanks for folks like Jim —
They do a lot for the rest of us,
Don't they?

3. The 'Holy' Me

Today
I find the idea of being good—attractive.
Today
I could forgive anyone, anything!
Today
I'm looking for ways to be helpful,
And what's more, I'm finding them!
Today
You could scratch my favourite LP
And I'd forgive you! Really I would!

What's the matter with me?

Whatever it is—
Thank You for this sudden influx
Of sweet reasonableness.
Mum's grateful for it!
And it must be a relief for You!

4. Just 'Reaction'

It's silly, really . . .
But life seems to have gone a bit tame,
Suddenly !
Nothing seems to be happening—
And the days are just dragging on—
Work and home, work and home . . . work and home . . .

Mum says I'm suffering from 'reaction'
After the busy time of working for the exams,
Winding up my work at school
And the first days at work !
And, I suppose she's right, really—
But these kind of days are hard to take.

I guess it's a case of plodding on !
Keeping going !
You might call it—ticking over !
I need to work at this kind of thing—
Don't I ?
I mean—I'm fine when it's all happening . . .

So, if You could help me brighten up a bit—
I'd appreciate it !

5. *Thoughts About Sex*

I'm not a prude—
You know that, don't You?
But—honestly, sometimes I feel funny about being a girl!
I don't think anything should make me feel like that—
Do You?

Am I right . . . or wrong?
I don't want to be a fuddy-duddy
Or old-fashioned—but, frankly,
I'm a bit sick of it all!

I'm not daft . . . either!
I know that sex is a very important part of life,
And I want to know about it,
And, when I'm ready,
Make a good marriage relationship.
But I think it's a very personal thing
And there's just too much sharing of very personal things
With the world at large
Nowadays . . . Don't You think so?

I mean—I think what my Mum says is probably quite right,
(And that's unusual, isn't it?)
Soon there will be nothing left to surprise us,
Delight us, or cause us to wonder.
I don't honestly think I want my life to be like that.
It sounds a bore, doesn't it?
Perhaps that's where we've gone wrong!

All I know is . . .
It's all too blasé for me.
I feel uncomfortable and embarrassed.

I think the others at school know I feel like this—
But I'm worried for them.
(I must sound like an old granny but I can't help it!)
They're getting far too caught up in this kind of thing . . .
I wouldn't like to say for certain—
But I'm pretty sure some of them
Have been to see some 'blue' films—
And there's always a bunch of pictures doing the rounds.

I don't think I've got a hope
But I wish I could help them to see
There's much more to relationships
Than just physical things . . .
But when I try to say it
It all comes out sounding trite and old-fashioned.

Help me to have the guts to find a way to say it—
Will You?

6. *Fear*

I had a grotty experience today.
I hadn't realized what a terrible thing fear is ...

Actually it was a very near scrape in the car.
For a moment, things hung in the balance
And I can't forget how I felt!

I was sickeningly afraid—
The sweat stood out on my forehead,
And my heart beat a tattoo
Which didn't make me feel any better!
I shrieked and clutched at the arm of the driver—
Then, suddenly, everything went into slow motion ...
And it was over;
But I shan't forget ... ever!

I wondered about other folk
Who had felt similar things—
Folks in an aircraft about to crash-land!
Soldiers going over the top into battle!
People who get shot in cold blood—
Because it's happening all the time, isn't it?

It's the nearest I've ever been to facing real fear
And it's made me think ... really think!

Life is very precious, isn't it?

7. Escape

Have You noticed that I'm here ... ?
I've been waiting for something from You, please—

OK, so I'm running away—
But at least I'm running to You, aren't I?

No, I can't go back and face it all—it's too awful!
You can't possibly understand if You make me go back.

It's impossible—it's just not on, not on at all;
They make me sick ... yes, sick!
Right down to the pit of my stomach—
(Yes, I know it's not a nice expression,
Well, it's not a nice feeling, either!)

I'm not trying to dodge it—
No I'm not. (If You'll listen I'll try to explain.)
I just feel that the most dignified thing to do
In this situation ... is ... withdraw!
(You're wrong ... it's not an excuse.)
I really feel that way ...
No!
I haven't conditioned myself to that way of thinking—
There is simply no place for me there, any more.
They don't want me, they've made it quite plain
(Even You must admit that!)

It's not good for them that I stay—
If I do—
They'll think they can do whatever they like to me
And get away with it ... and they'll be right!

No ... (with respect, I think You're wrong!)
I don't think they do need me!
(Oh, it's all right ... I know what You're trying to say
    to me—
But I'm not buying it!)
(SILENCE)

Well ... just suppose they really don't understand
That they need me. (I'll give You that!)
Just where do we go from here?
I can't take any more.
(All right, all right, I know that's the real problem—
Please don't rub it in ...)
That's what hurts really!
I just can't take it ...
I don't have that kind of strength ...
(SILENCE)

All right . . pour Your strength into me!
Yes, I know You can do it—
I do, really—
So
Please—
Lift me up into Your vast reservoir of strength
And guts and courage—
And soak me in it!
It's the only way I'm going to be able to go back!

8. Escaping — Facing Up

Well, here I am—
Back!
It's a bit of a let-down, actually!
I wish I could hold on to that high moment
When You stiffened me up to come back—
But I've lost all sense of it.
And now ... here ... on my own ...
Waiting for the first brush with them—
I feel a bit washed-out and deflated!
(Yes, You're right—I'm tired,
Actually I feel quite drained and exhausted.)

Well, I don't know what I expected
But it's obviously not going to be anything dramatic,
Is it?

So ... I'd better get on with it!
(Stay around, please ... it's the least You can do!)
Remember—I'm relying on *You*!)

9. On Being 'Bomb-Happy'

Whooooooooooo-pee!
I'm dancing into Your presence today!
Don't ask me why—I don't know
I just feel 'bomb-happy', somehow!

No—nothing has gone particularly right—
But then, nothing has gone particularly wrong, either.
I just woke up with this feeling of content—
No, it's more than that...
It's a feeling that everything in the world is fine:
I'm fine, life is fine... it's all fine!

Aren't we funny people?
Yesterday I was full of myself, and problems—
It all sat on me like a big fog cloud—
But, today...
Well, today is another story.

I guess You'll say there's something to watch here,
Won't You?
And, as usual, You'll be right.
(If I'm honest, I can see it, too!)
After all, if I go on like this
I'll drive myself and everybody else—mad!

(Mum's always saying I ought to learn a little balance in
    life!)
Well, I will be balanced—I will... I will... I will!
Only today—I feel 'bomb-happy'.

10. Sunday Blues

It's Sunday
And I don't feel remotely like it . . . at all !
I felt more like praying at the football match, yesterday
When our kid scored the equaliser !
I could have shouted Your praise till I burst —
But not today !
Today, the thought of sermons and songs
Turns me off —
Not on !

Could you take yesterday's moment then,
In lieu of today ?
I've a feeling it will suit You more
Than the buttoned-up attention
I'll have to turn on today.
That isn't really me, You know !
Yesterday was what I really wanted
You to know !

11. On Being Fed-up

I'm fed-up!

Well, that's just it—I don't know why!
I feel as though I'm sickening for something,
Only not like measles or anything,
It's like having a blight on my spirit!

I just can't beat it—
I've tried every way.
Mum coughed up for a new pair of shoes
And that helped for a while,
Until I saw that girl I can't stick, down the road
Wearing a pair exactly the same.
I went off them!
And Mum's cross now—
Says it's a waste of money.
(Yes, I thought You'd think it was, too.
Well, maybe I'll wear them,
Just to please You!)

12. Everything Getting On Your Nerves

I can't do with noise today . . .
My ears feel as though they belong to an elephant,
As though they are made of sponge
Soaking up every sound.
Things are getting on my nerves
Gradually.
Small things,
Things I suppose I wouldn't notice normally
But, today . . .

I've been told that I got out of bed the wrong side,
That I'm in one of my moods,
And a whole host of other things
That don't help at all.

I've a feeling this is a You situation—
So I'm sending help signals.
This is what I need—
Calm
      Poise
           Graciousness.
That's a tall order, I know,
But I've a feeling You can cope!

13. On Being Let Down, Seemingly

It was important to me, You know!
It might have seemed small to him
But it was big for me,
And I needed to get it off my chest to someone.
I can't understand him!
I've always thought such a lot of him.
He was great to me when I boobed my 'O' levels—
In fact he was the only one who didn't say
'Never mind, son, you can always try again next year!'
Because that wasn't the point :
It was just terrible to have failed this year!
So what was the matter with him the other night?
Pam only wanted to talk to him about the Youth Club
    outing—
I needed him—
Why didn't he see that?
Well, I'm sorry but I think he let me down—badly!

You had time for people, didn't You?
You didn't push them off with a casual
'Can I see you another time, Tom?'
Well, then . . . he's supposed to be being like You
Isn't he?

All right, so I'm shouting. Sorry!
OK, I'll calm down! Not that I'm het-up, really,
Well, all right then . . . just a bit het-up!
I just can't seem to get over it, that's all!

What do You mean? I'll see it differently in a little while?
How can it change? It happened, didn't it?
Oh, I see—it's the old one—
I'll change !
Well, I don't know that I will !
Yes I know I'm up one minute and down the next ...
And the next time he does something I approve of
He'll be the 'greatest' again.
So ... You've talked me into it ... haven't You?

14. Jealousy

I feel awful!
Sick!
I wouldn't tell everyone, but I cried myself to sleep last
    night;
(Well, how would You feel—if you saw someone else being
    given
All the things you wanted? Things you'd give your eye-teeth
    to have! And what's more, taking it all for granted!)
Life's not fair, You know!
Just not fair!

The worst of it is
The things I have got—I don't want any more!
I've gone off them! It's taken all my pleasure in them,
    away
And I just can't forgive that!
It's all spoiled ... somehow!

I hate him ...
He's got everything—good looks, personality, ability,
And money!
His Mum and Dad think the light shines out of him—
Honestly ... it makes you sick!

Mum says I've got to come to terms with it;
(Incidentally, I don't know how she knows, but she'd
    twigged it somehow!)

She says I've got to be thankful for being me;
And learn to know myself, and face the fact that
He's just that much better on some things!
(Well it's not some things . . . it's most things!)
She says it's part of growing up—becoming mature,
That it happens to everyone!
(Well, I bet it doesn't happen to him!)

I can't help it! I don't feel mature!
I just feel physically sick, and hurt and upset
And the world has gone sour!
I wouldn't care if it had been fair.
But no one even looked at the work I had put in,
The hours I had spent, the times I'd carried on when
No one else would do it!
No . . . they just voted him in! Full stop!
And he hasn't been here five minutes!

Well, I just know that if You can't help me in this
Then I'm sunk!
And I know that if I can't lick this
I'll never lick anything!
And what's more . . . somehow, I've got to work with him!

God, You are so big . . .
I feel exhausted—drained of strength—no feelings
    any more—
Pick me up and hold me,
I'm sore all over, in my spirit—
Be gentle with me—
Just, kind of 'love me' a bit . . .
Just until I can manage to get going again!

15. Feeling Chuffed

I feel really chuffed (I thought You'd like to know!)
Well, I can't really let on to anyone else—
After all it's not the thing to show that you're chuffed
About something.
Oh no . . . you're supposed to meet the whole thing
With a deadpan face;
Don't let on . . . it's the 'in' thing.
You see, if someone knows you're pleased
Then, ten-to-one, they try to spoil it for you!
It seems a built-in part of human nature.
They can't wait to prick the bubble
To bring you down! People are like that—You know!

Anyhow, it's important to keep it to yourself!
But I'd like You to know that I'm chuffed,
Pleased—actually, to be honest—
Over the moon. I feel great, tremendous, fantastic!
Couldn't be better!
I suppose You'll be wanting to know what it's all about.
Well . . . wait for it . . .
I actually passed—in maths . . . imagine! Me!
I actually went out there . . . and passed!
I expected to get through the other subjects, but . . . maths!
Wow! You should have seen my teacher's face!
He was knocked-out!

I think Mum's guessed how chuffed I am;
I don't seem to be able to keep it from her, somehow—
She always knows!

16. Deflation

Well ... I've just had my bubble well and truly pricked !
I went in, full of zest and enthusiasm,
And came out with my tail between my legs.

I wouldn't care if anything I'd done was intentional—
It never is !
I make mistakes ... like everyone else in Your world,
Or so I thought.
Now—I'm rapidly coming to the conclusion
That there are those (a race apart)
Who never make mistakes.

It's not a nice feeling, You know—
It isn't that I mind being told,
It's just that it takes the joy out of it all,
Somehow the light goes out ... and with it ... the
    inspiration !

Do they have a right to do this ?
Those who sit in heavy authority upon us ...
Are You pleased with it all—
Or are You still hoping that somewhere, sometime,
The gentle fingers of understanding
Will temper that word of reproof ?

I don't mind ... honestly I don't
(Don't worry about me, please !).
It's just that they'll never know
How it saps my energies ...
And quenches my spirit (for a while !) :

17. Laughter

I feel a bit bad—
And I don't think You're going to like it much
Either!
I've just laughed in the wrong place.
(No, that doesn't sound too great a crime,
I agree ... but wait till I explain.)
I think we were all a bit insensitive, really,
But, I agree
That doesn't excuse me!

We'd asked for ideas—readings and poems
And that kind of thing
For the next issue of the mag.!
I'd forgotten Joan fancies herself as a bit of a poet.
Well, the others really took the mickey ...
And I must confess I thought it was a bit of a giggle
Myself! That is ... until I saw her face!

This 'laughter' thing can go so wrong,
Can't it?
I'm sorry ... really, I am.
(Must I say sorry to Joan as well?)
Yes ... I thought You'd say that!

18. Desperation

Judy's desperate . . . and it's awful!
Really it is!
I can't seem to get near her at all.
She's just gone right inside herself somewhere
Where I can't follow!
Fortunately I had the great idea
Of bringing her home and leaving her alone
With my Dad . . . to talk!
(He's good at that kind of thing, You know!)
Well, she looked happier . . . later on!
But, I just couldn't understand it all!
How can you get to that state?
Why don't you do something before you get there?
It's all a great puzzle to me . . . really it is.
(SILENCE)

Yes, I suppose You are right.
It is difficult to understand something
When you've never experienced it yourself.
I suppose I'll just have to go on . . . being . . . around . . .
Without understanding.
Just available.

19. Sense of Humour

Some folk are great, aren't they?
You just can't quench them.
We were waiting for the bus tonight—
There was quite a queue.
It was belting it down with rain;
We were all pretty wet,
And more than a bit miserable,
Not a bus for twelve minutes!

Then one came.
The conductor was a little cockney fellow,
He leaned out from his platform
Beaming all over his face, and called,
'Come on, you lot;
In twos then . . . all aboard the Ark.'
Well, we had to laugh,
We couldn't help ourselves!

You certainly knew what You were doing
When You gave us a sense of humour!

20. Ambition

It's only natural to want to get on,
Isn't it?
There's nothing wrong in it ... is there?
To do reasonably well
Whatever job you decide to spend your life doing?

Only I don't like some of it, somehow!
I don't like it when it means
Climbing and clambering over other folks
To get somewhere.
People do it, don't they?
You see it happening all the time ...
There's nothing of 'loving your neighbour as yourself'
In that, is there?

Do You know what I think?
I think we sometimes kid ourselves
That it doesn't matter,
Those of us who are supposed to be Christian.

It's important to know it matters, though,
Isn't it?

21. Prejudice

I've been trying to kid myself all week
That I'm never prejudiced;
Oh, I don't mean about the black and white business,
And all that! That's old hat now.
No, I mean about everything in life.
You know—
What other folk can do, and do well,
Perhaps better than I can!
It's all right with the people you like, you know.
It's the ones you don't much care for,
They're the problem!
It's difficult to be enthusiastic about them,
Isn't it?
They might have the most terrific talent,
Or might achieve the most spectacular things ...
But somehow, you can't be generous about it!
I know it's not very attractive to be like this,
But, sometimes, I just can't seem to help it!

I want to, though ...
And I'll keep going at it,
If You'll keep understanding!

22. *Being Praised*

I feel full of sweetness and light...
How about that?
I've actually done something right, for a change!
I said the right thing, to the right person,
At the right moment—
And you can't get better than that
Can you?
Dad said (listen to this)—Dad said
He was proud of me,
And Gran beamed all over her face!

OK I know I'm being sickening;
If it was anyone else
I'd want to say, Yuuuuuuuk!
But, just this once
I'm going to wallow in it!
After all
It doesn't happen very often, does it?
Even You must be hard put to it
To remember the last time!
And I'm sure I wouldn't have missed out
On telling You!

VI

Shout Prayers

I'm furious, livid!	People who should know better are sticking their heads in the ground like ostriches, and refusing to see. Help me, Lord.
I'm concerned	The spirit amongst a group of Christians I know is all wrong, somehow . . . Help me to pray constructively for them.
I'm amazed	Someone I've known all my life has just taken deliberate advantage of me. I just can't believe it! Help me assess this properly, please.
I'm shattered	After all I've done for her, she's gone off with someone else. Help me to understand.
I'm annoyed	I've been left with all the hard work to do again . . . again . . . again . . . Help me do it, please.
I'm afraid	I know this is going to be a bad week. I don't want to mess it up! Strengthen me, please.
I'm exasperated	My patience is exhausted. I've tried everything, but they don't want to learn! Help me, please.
I'm upset	I planned it all so well, and they've bungled it for me. Help me, please.
I'm tired	And I'm going to bite someone's head off, if I'm not careful. Help me, please.

I'm excited	And it's going to my head. Keep my feet on the ground, please.
I'm anxious	I want to do well, and it means a lot to the others too. Give me a hand, please.
I'm flabbergasted	They just don't care. Do they? Please stretch my patience a little further.
I'm frantic with	Someone I love is ill and I can't help them. Please surround us with Your Love.

VII

Thank You Prayers

Thank you   For surprises, especially on dull days.
For smiles . . . they don't cost anything but they're worth their weight in gold.
For kindred spirits.
For jokes . . . the kind ones !
For people who love me, even when I don't deserve it !
For colour . . . in contrast.
For beauty of design and form.
For animals who share our lives, without demanding anything in return.
For the sense of touch, and the rough, smooth, texture of things.
For raindrops on the petals of flowers.
For sensitive people, who see more clearly than I do.
For the clear, cool air of moorlands, and hills.
For love, and the way it enriches life.
For strength and a healthy body.
For children . . . especially babies.
For music . . . and music . . . and music.
For a line of washing dancing in the breeze.
For rain.
For the sense of smell, especially Sunday lunchtime.
For laughter and the way it charms you away from a bad mood.
For warmth, especially on a winter day.

Thank you   For birds . . . birds . . . birds . . . especially blackbirds.

For the ability to sense You . . . and enjoy Your presence.

For home.

For work to do.

For everything that tests me . . . and shows what I'm made of.

For incentives.

For scientists and technicians, who make our world interesting.

For creative minds.

For books and reading.

For the sense of taste, especially at Christmas.

For birthdays.

For small things that bring pleasure, and the ability to enjoy them.

For art.

For friendship, that survives all sorts of things.

For worship, especially when in the company of likeminded people.

For a sense of Eternity.

For poetry.

For choice . . . even when it's difficult.